No Limits

No Limits

Al Foxx

Winners Don't Quit Association
Woodinville, WA

NO LIMITS

Published by the Winners Don't Quit Association

President of the Winners Don't Quit Association
www.alfoxx.com

ISBN: 978-0-9783781-3-4

Winners Don't Quit Association
PO Box 2347
Woodinville WA 98072
~~1-888-550-FOXX~~ 425-820-0367
~~1-888-550-3699~~
~~bookings@alfoxx.com~~
~~www.winnersdontquit.org~~
alfoxx@alfoxx.com
www.alfoxx.com

WDQ
al foxx

Table of Contents

You've no doubt faced many obstacles and limitations in your life. These pages describe some of the limitations I've faced during the last twenty-one years of my rehabilitation, plus many of the serious and humorous situations I've encountered. Normally, rehabilitation floors and psychologists' offices are heavy and void of humor. But, as we all know, laughter is the best medicine—and it's one of the most valuable forms of therapy.

It took me several years of living with brain damage and a half-paralyzed body to be comfortable enough to laugh at my limits. I encourage you to laugh along with me—with me, not at me. No one enjoys being laughed at. In fact, my disability makes some people in comedy clubs where I perform feel uneasy when I first hobble on stage.

As I open my mouth, audiences see how comfortable I am and they relax. Then they wonder if I'm faking it. On more than one occasion people have come up to me after a show and asked if my "apparent" disability is part of my act. "Just between you and me," I say confidentially, "I'm faking it. When I go home, I start walking normal."

I believe we're in bondage to what we can't laugh at. Laughing at something makes it less overwhelming and more manageable.

My hope is that by reading this book, you will gain the courage to face the limits and obstacles life sends your way. I know that with faith in yourself—and in the highest powers—you too can have the confidence to never give up, to keep on winning, to believe that there really are no limits.

It's all a matter of choice. Choose possibilities. Keep smiling.

—Al Foxx

Chapter 1

What Speed Limit?

There is more to life than increasing its speed.
—Gandhi

Do you remember when you were nineteen years old? When I was nineteen, I loved cars and motorcycles and one special gal. My job as a hot-tar roofer earned me enough money to customize my Camaro and buy a brand new Yamaha 650 Special. To make life even sweeter, I had a gorgeous girlfriend named Cheryl who wore my diamond engagement ring. She loved to ride on the back of my bike, her arms wrapped around my waist, and her golden hair flying behind us.

On May 7, 1980, a friend and I planned to meet after work and go to a Van Halen concert. I stopped by Cheryl's house on the way. Time flew by whenever we were together, and before I realized it, I was late for the concert. I jumped on my bike, gunned out of the driveway and raced down the street. Wind screamed past my helmet and tore at my leather jacket. I should have slowed down, but I sped up. The orange speedometer needle climbed toward vertical.

I loved the wind in my face. I gave my bike more gas. I felt free, happy, and powerful.

Wham!

I never saw the pick-up that ran a stop sign right in front of me. Judging from the distance that my bike knocked the truck, police say I was going over twice the speed limit. My bike hit the truck and stopped dead, I shot over the handlebars like I'd been fired from a circus cannon. My head slammed into the truck, cracking my helmet and breaking bones in my face. My limp body crumpled to the pavement. Someone called an ambulance.

My heart never quit beating, but because of massive internal hemorrhaging, my blood pressure was too low to read. Paramedics fit me with pressure pants to help squeeze blood from my legs toward my heart and head. Smooth and efficient as a Swiss watch, they laid me on a stretcher, loaded me in the van and raced to Harborview Hospital in Seattle. I was rushed into surgery where doctors removed my spleen and transfused seven and a half pints of blood into me.

No one knew if I would live or die. The pastor and his wife from my parents' church came to the hospital to be with my parents. A twenty-four-hour prayer vigil began among church members. After two weeks in critical care, I was still comatose, but my vitals had stabilized so they moved me into a private room. Because of the type of brain injury I'd sustained, a doctor told my parents to start looking for a convalescent home. The hospital would have to move me if I didn't wake up within two weeks. I'm told that when my primary-care physician heard what they told my parents, he erupted in anger.

I'm not sure if he got mad because he was the one responsible for making decisions about discharge, or because the other doctor's insensitivity made my parents suffer more than they had to. Either way, I whole-heartedly agree with his reported agitation. Why cause more suffering than there already was?

Tears flooded my mom's eyes and ran down her cheeks as I lay in ICU. The doctor told her, "Even if he lives, he'll never be the same." Physically and mentally, she was warned, I would be a different person. And there would be behavior changes, maybe drastic changes.

Several years ago, I discovered that my mom had kept a poetic journal of her thoughts during this period. She sent me these lines that I think of as a …

Mother's Prayer

I'm sorry Lord.
I thought I was strong—
I thought I was prepared to face the worst.
When the doctor told me he would never be the same

that his intelligence would not
reach the same level as before the accident
that there would be behavior modifications—
I knew You were still in control.
That out of tragedies, blessings come
that no matter what happens
You can take that thing—
that hurt—and turn it into
something good—turn it into a blessing.

My parents' trust that God would bring blessings out of tragedies gave me courage even though, at the time, I felt nothing but contempt for God. Their conviction that God could rebuild a crushed life gave them strength. Their strength gave me hope. But they were only human. I can't even imagine how they felt when the doctors told them they'd have to start looking for a convalescent home if I didn't wake up soon. My mother continued:

The doctor's words kept coming back—
He won't be the same—
He may need 24-hour nursing care
When he leaves here—
You aren't obligated to take care of him
The rest of his life—
But it's too early to tell.
We don't know how much damage was done to the brain.

Two weeks later, a month after my accident, I began waking up from my coma. Sometimes people wake up violently. My waking up process was slow and gentle. I gradually became aware of my surroundings. Because of paralysis, during the coma my vocal chords fused together. I sounded like a cross between Sasquatch and a cave man.

I was the emotional and mental age of an infant. A female therapist would hold up a card with a word printed on it, like "mom" or "home." I would reach out and touch the card then look at her for approval.

That look in his eyes—that longing, forlorn look as with effort he formed the word "home," the word he had repeated so often the last few days.
At first he could only searchingly point to the letters on the card:
H-O-M-E.
Then slowly the sound became intelligent.
Yes, I want to take you home.
My heart aches when I see your longing eyes,
your trusting face.
Is this why God saved your life?
Is this what God wants me to do
with my time and energy—
to take care of a little boy—
a trusting little boy
who just before his nineteenth
birthday was a strong, healthy,
active, handsome, young man?
You don't remember your birthday—
we sang to you as you lay in a coma in ICU.

I was so disoriented I didn't know up from down. When they raised the head of my bed, my head plopped to the side. When they'd put me in a wheelchair, I'd flop out like a big dead fish. For weeks, I had to wear a halo attached to my wheelchair. A halo is a vertical bar fastened to the back of a wheelchair, projecting a bit higher than the patient's head. A strap is fastened to the top end of the bar and wrapped around the patient's head so it doesn't flop to the side and pull the person out of the chair.

Partly because of my head injury and partly because of the many painkillers I was on, I didn't know how bad things were. About three months after my injury, I realized with wrecking-ball abruptness just how much things had changed.

Chapter 2

Never Walk? Never Drive?

Pain is inevitable. Suffering is optional.
—M. Kathleen Casey

Have you ever asked for something you ended up not wanting? I not only asked to see Harborview Hospital's chief neurosurgeon, I insisted on it. Finally he visited my room. He was a big rough-looking man, but as he stood beside my bed, he looked more like a truant student called into the principal's office. My speech was garbled. I had to point to letters on an alphabet board to ask him how long he thought it would take before I could walk and drive again.

The noises coming from the hospital hallway seemed to fall silent. I held my breath. My beating heart pounded nails into my coffin. Why didn't he answer? His eyes went from looking at the alphabet board to my face as he slowly told me, "You will never be able to walk or drive again."

I panicked.

Never walk? Never drive? I'm a nineteen-year-old roofer. I have to walk! I have to drive! Talk about being handed a set of limits. Frantically, I pushed my paralyzed leg off the bed and tried to stand up. Why was the room tilted? I reached out to balance myself on the bedside table, but I missed and fell on my face. The doctor and two nurses put me back in bed like I was some kind of weak, disease-ravished old man. How humiliating! I couldn't have that. As soon as they turned around, I climbed back out and fell on my face again. This time they put me back and strapped me in.

As I lay there staring at the ceiling, I could see the writing on the wall (which is quite a feat). The belt strapping me to the bed was redundant. Horror at what lay ahead kept me frozen to the mattress. I was too scared to even think about the changes I faced, but an invisible force pulled my mind to where it had never gone before.

The handwriting on the wall stood out clearly; instead of hanging out with friends—backpacking, parachuting, snow and water skiing, going to rock concerts and to the beach—I'd be spending my time in therapy: physical, speech, occupational, and psychotherapy. What kind of life was that? I had always pitied people who had life-changing accidents. I could never even imagine it happening to me, but now it had. The impossible had happened: I was handed a life-sentence of limitations. How would I react?

Life since my motorcycle crash has been unlike anything I have ever known. Having my strong, capable body replaced by a shell of what it had been was like being plucked from a jungle of luscious, colorful fruit and thrown into a desert of heat-blasted sand.

Even more dramatic were the changes going on inside my head. My thoughts used to arrive with the speed of Indy cars. Now they arrived with the sluggishness of covered wagons on the Oregon Trail.

Looking back, there is no way I could have come this far if it hadn't been for key people to guide me around pitfalls. I haven't always listened to the guides, but as time and troubles have passed, I've become more willing to heed the advice of those who have gone before me.

At Harborview, nothing mattered but my memory of the great life I'd enjoyed. The doctor's words echoed in my ears: "Never walk or drive again." The dismal future I faced glowed on the wall where the bloodless hand had written its prediction. My life had exploded like a torpedoed battleship. All that remained were bubbles floating on the ocean's surface—the ocean of my life.

All the things that had made me feel like a winner were gone! No high-paying job, no customized Camaro, no beautiful motorcycle. I couldn't even get out of bed. Any possessions I owned were meaningless since I couldn't use them anymore. My once strong athletic body was a now a useless pile of muscles and bones. My gorgeous fiancée was all that remained of the life I'd enjoyed. I loved her before my accident when I was strong and independent. Now my love changed to a devouring need unlike any I'd ever known. I clung to her like a man clinging to a rope over a tank of hungry sharks.

Chapter 3

Rehabilitation 101

Providence has hidden a charm in difficult undertakings which is appreciated only by those who dare to grapple with them.
—Anne-Sophie Swetchine

What is the best thing about life? To me, the best thing about life is being able to choose whether I want to be a winner or a loser. Losers see calamities and limitations everywhere they look. Winners, on the other hand, see challenges and possibilities everywhere they look.

Rehabilitation has been a series of challenges. My first goals after waking from the coma sound simpler than they actually were. Things like learning to sit in a wheelchair without my head flopping to the side. Learning to pull on my socks and tie my shoes with my one good hand. Learning to hold my water till I reached the bathroom was a big deal at the time. Goals like these filled my days at the beginning of my rehabilitation.

At first glance, the physical goals facing me seemed tough. But a tougher, more elusive goal was keeping my spirits up. How can you be happy when you've gone from having the kind of life every nineteen-year-old wants to having the kind of life no nineteen-year-old wants?

Rehabilitation seemed impossible at first, but as they say, "Necessity is the mother of invention." Over time, I discovered ways to build and maintain a positive spirit. When I'm in high spirits, I feel as if I can do anything. But if my spirits are down, even routine obstacles seem insurmountable.

The condition of my body has had a huge impact on my spirit. I feel best when I get physical exercise, plenty of sleep, and eat wholesome food.

My head injury ruptured my brain stem, which serves as a type of control tower that sends messages to individual muscles. The muscles on my left side were intact, but they wouldn't move because they weren't receiving any messages from the control tower. Even worse, my hypothalamus gland ruptured. The hypothalamus helps regulate and stabilize emotions.

Sun streamed through the open window and fresh air filled the hospital's Physical Therapy Room as I lay on my back on the PT mat and Cynthia, my therapist, knelt beside me and held my elbow.

"Al," she said, "let me see you straighten your arm." I didn't expect it to budge. It hadn't moved last time or the time before that, but I gave it a shot. My mouth popped open as my arm straightened and my hand rose toward the ceiling. I was shocked! Part of my triceps had heard the command to move.

I wish Cynthia had been able to work her magic on the rest of my muscles or on my ruptured hypothalamus. Interacting normally with people is tough when you erupt like a volcano without warning. As a matter of fact, Mount St. Helens erupted on May 18, 1980, just eleven days after my accident. Coincidence?

One of my first limits was not being able to walk. My goal became to walk using a specially made walker with one handle in the middle. Once I learned to use the walker to totter across the physical therapy room, my next goal was to hobble down the hall to the office where I took speech therapy.

One day, with me gripping the walker and my fiancée gripping the belt around my waist, my physical therapist walked behind us pushing my wheelchair giving instructions like, "Stand straighter. Take the same size steps with both feet. Slow down. Stop kissing your girlfriend!"

Why?

Even with someone helping me keep my balance and me leaning on the walker, it still took a couple months of trying before I could cover the 30 yards from the PT room to the speech therapy office. I can still remember how proud I felt the first time I made it.

I remembered how in the not-too-distant past I had carried a full backpack 25 miles over hilly terrain and now I was struggling to hobble down a short hallway. What was wrong with me? I felt okay. Why wouldn't my muscles do what I told them? I couldn't have made it without using that walker and having someone holding my safety belt. I hated that walker. Once, I hurled it across the PT room. It crashed into the wall and clattered to the floor.

Taking two months to build up to hobbling all the way down the hall doesn't seem like much of an accomplishment. But looking back on it now, twenty-one years later, those two months seem incredible. I spent the first year after I was out of the hospital making the shift from a quad-cane to a one-point cane. I spent the next sixteen years learning to walk with no cane at all. Two months were nothing.

Because my vocal chords had fused together during the coma, my voice sounded like a jammed chainsaw. Talk about embarrassing! I had to repeat myself again and again. I'd get super mad. People thought I was angry with them when I was just mad at my situation. Back in the hospital, a speech therapist helped my enunciation by having me repeat short phrases over and over, emphasizing a different word each time. Her favorite phrase to repeat was: "WINNERS Don't Quit! Winners DON'T Quit!! Winners Don't QUIT!!!"

I took physical and speech therapy for seven years. The therapists I saw after getting out of the hospital had me recite words and phrases into a tape recorder. Not only did the tape help me adjust the way I sounded, but analyzing my speech helped me notice that I was actually getting better. Setting goals and tracking my progress at overcoming limits raised my spirits.

While in the hospital, my speech impairment was so bad that when hospital visitors heard my barking, they thought they were in the Seattle Aquarium. A few other patients at the time had similar speech impairments.

One night I dreamed that four of us were sitting in the lobby by the nurse's desk impatiently waiting for our afternoon snacks. A young woman stepped off the elevator and heard us barking away. She got excited and pulled her husband toward us. "Come on, Honey, let's feed the seals." The reason I remember this is because she happened to have a purse full of freshly caught fish. She pulled them out one by one and started tossing them to us. Our wheelchairs crashed together as we raced around with our mouths wide open. A few fish hit the floor, but we caught most of them. We didn't complain that our snacks were late.

At age eighteen, I saw myself as a confident winner. At nineteen, I saw myself as a complete loser. And because I saw myself as a loser, I was a loser. Over the years, I've realized that just because everything was going my way when I was eighteen didn't mean I was a winner. And just because nothing seemed to be going my way when I was nineteen didn't mean I was a loser.

Life's circumstances don't determine a person's value. How we choose to see life's circumstances is what makes us winners or losers. Losers see calamities in every challenge. Winners see challenges in every calamity.

Whether I choose to see challenges or calamities is entirely up to me.

Choices are the most powerful freedom we have. Choices will either make us or break us. One choice at a time, we're either building our castle or our coffin. A scary thing about choices is that it takes a whole series of good choices to improve your life, but only one bad choice can destroy your life. It did mine.

During my time in the hospital and for the first year after being released, I wanted my fiancée Cheryl to be with me constantly. If I knew then what I know now, I wouldn't have asked her to spend so much time with me. If she hadn't spent so much time with me, and if I'd walked through more of my "fire" alone, things might have worked out better between us.

Instead of basing my self-acceptance on how I thought someone else felt about me, I had to come to grips with how I felt about the new me. The problem was that part of my fire was my fear of being alone. And because I couldn't find the courage to face my fear, I discovered what it means to be really alone.

My fear of being left alone overpowered the confidence I'd known. I wanted to be with Cheryl not just because I loved her, but also because of my deep hunger that I thought only she could satisfy. Because of my hunger and my dependence on her, I was happy only until she had to leave. Then I was right back where I started—alone and miserable. When I quit looking outside myself, when I became comfortable with whom I'd become, I began building healthy relationships and finding true happiness.

As I eventually discovered, when you mix physical love into a relationship where neither party is emotionally ready for it, you're asking for disaster. Cheryl was great to be around, but being with me was hard on her. Sometimes she cried. Being with her was hard for me, too. I hated to see her cry. I felt responsible, but what could I do?

If only I knew then what I know now, how different things could have been. If only I'd known that we each had a fire to walk through. If only I'd known that we each had to face our fires alone. If only I'd known.

My highest hope is that some of the thousands of people who go through what I did will learn from my experience. I don't mean to sound like some kind of all-knowing guru. I'm not.

What I know is that we all learn different things in different ways, depending on the path we travel. For your sake, I hope you are able to pass on some of what your path has taught you. If we all pass on what can help others, we will all be wiser and happier.

Chapter 4

A Lesson in Love

Love can sweep you off your feet and carry you along in a way you've never known before. But the ride always ends, and you end up feeling lonely and bitter. Wait. It's not love I'm describing. I'm thinking of a monorail.

—Jack Handey

Sweetie, I love you," Cheryl said. Thick lashes surrounded Cheryl's big brown eyes. Her eyes took away my fears. What she said made me feel like I could do anything. But whenever she'd leave, and we were no longer physically together, what worried me was that I wasn't the same person she had once agreed to marry. I loved her so much it hurt, but my feelings for her were like an iron necklace—a necklace of fear. She was a beautiful woman who could have her pick of guys. Why would she want a cripple? She seemed fine with it right then, but how long would it last? There are plenty of guys who have it together so much better than I do, who would jump at the chance to be with her.

Cheryl was the last vestige of the life I'd loved. I clung to her as if she was a life preserver and I was a man who'd been knocked off the deck of his battleship. Everywhere I looked, seemingly insurmountable obstacles—like relearning to talk, walk, drive, dress, feed myself—took on the shape of hungry sharks. Sharks that seemed determined to keep me from becoming the type of man every beautiful young woman wants and deserves.

"I love you, too, Babe," I said. Cheryl sat in a chair facing my wheelchair and I leaned forward far enough to kiss her soft lips.

After I came out of my coma, and once I could understand what he was talking about, my psychologist warned my fiancée and me that I wasn't emotionally capable of understanding and dealing with the feelings that accompany a physical relationship. Did we listen? No.

That was one of the best pieces of advice I ever ignored.

Intellectually, I was slow, but I could still understand what he said. My problem was that physically I was a young man, but emotionally I was an infant. Our intellect, physical desires, and emotional maturity are completely separate. Even an intellectual or physical giant can be as emotionally immature as a toddler.

"Come on, Cheryl. We're gonna do it all the time after we get married. What difference does it make if we begin a little early?" I was probably the first guy in the history of the world to use that line. Not!

My accident had been too recent to add any maturity to either of us. Being reckless and rebellious, Cheryl and I both thought we knew enough to ignore the advice of the psychologist. Another problem I glimpsed early on but was too afraid to acknowledge was that she could just up and walk away, which she eventually did, leaving me behind to deal with the results of our reckless behavior. How can something that started so sweet turn so bitter?

As Albert Einstein wrote: "How on earth are you ever going to explain in terms of chemistry and physics so important a biological phenomenon as first love?"

Just like a sexually abused kid, the results of our irresponsible behavior took years of counseling and uncomfortable effort to eradicate. The process cost me time, money, embarrassment, broken relationships, and tons of heartache.

I paid a price for ignoring the psychologist's advice. I could not walk away from what had happened. My mind was as impressionable as a child's in the same way that a child's earliest experiences influence what the adult considers normal later in life. My fiancée's and my behavior cut psychological tracks in my thinking that took nearly two decades of on again, off again counseling to erase.

More than a few psychologists told me that I was having problems with relationships because I was unconsciously using the same behaviors that had been successful with Cheryl with every new girl I met. I was embarrassed at my behavior and intimidated by the enormity of its psychological causes. I couldn't even think of including this aspect of my rehabilitation in my talks to students in school assemblies, or in this book, or even in my stand-up comedy routine until counseling helped me eliminate the problem and strengthen my crumbling self-esteem.

Today, I earn my living sharing what a traumatic brain injury and twenty-one years of rehabilitation has taught me. It would now be unthinkable to not mention the havoc that having sex before I was psychologically and emotionally ready cost me. It destroyed my social life for almost twenty years! For nearly two decades I was in and out of counseling sessions to help me maintain healthy relationships. In the past year, I have established and am maintaining more healthy relationships than I did in the first twenty years following my motorcycle crash. I've set and reached a ton of goals since my injury, but rediscovering that women can be colleagues and friends is one of my most valuable and enjoyable rehabilitative victories.

As I look back on my relationship with Cheryl from the comfort of a rebuilt life, I'm sure it was a combination of things that tore us apart. More than anything, it was the change in my attitude that led to our separation. The combination of losing everything I had, plus losing my ability to get any of it back, changed me from a happy, confident young man to an angry, bitter person wrapped in self-pity.

Our attitude is one of the most powerful things we have. Attitude is a choice. The attitude we choose can either make us or break us; it will either build our castle or our coffin.

Painful as it was, my fiancée's leaving me was apparently typical. Broken relationships happen in the vast majority of cases involving life-altering injuries. I felt terrible that Cheryl left, but I also cherish the memories of the good times we shared before she was gone. I could have saved myself decades of pain and a score of friendships if only we'd listened and waited until we were both ready.

If you are in a similar situation and my experience helps you to wait, I'm glad I could help. If you're in a similar situation and hearing my experience doesn't make any difference to you, I understand. Some of us are destined to learn the hard way.

Chapter 5

An Evening With Bruce Springsteen

We don't like their sound, and guitar music is on the way out.
—Decca Recording Company, rejecting the Beatles, 1962

Have you ever been to a rock concert? My arm hung over Cheryl's shoulders as we made our way among the thousands of people waiting to see Bruce Springsteen in concert. The Boss! I'd seen him before my accident and I was psyched about seeing him again. Concerts had been a passion of mine ever since I saw my first Aerosmith show three or four years before. Eric Clapton, The Who, the Grateful Dead, the Doobie Brothers, Bad Company, and many others I saw were all good. But back in the late '70s and very early '80s, Bruce Springsteen was the Boss.

Hobbling along with Cheryl's help, most people probably thought I was too drunk to walk on my own. I know the police officers at the door to the coliseum thought I was. At least they thought I was until they tried to give me the typical search and Cheryl let them know right then what was up. They didn't search me. They didn't even search her, or my friend Joe Storm, who I had worked with as a roofer and who was walking with us into the concert. It always amazes me how much instant respect a fiery-eyed, gorgeous blonde can get from total strangers, especially when she's got the power of right on her side.

Joe and I had gone to a ton of concerts together before my accident. The Boss was one of a handful of bands you had to see at least twice. He put on a longer, harder rocking show than anyone I'd ever seen.

Springsteen's show had sold out, so we hadn't been able to get three seats together. We had two seats on the floor and one in the third row of the stands. Once inside, we made our way to the two seats on the floor. Joe, who had gotten the tickets, being his typical cool self, said to Cheryl, "You sit down here with Al. I'll sit in this other seat for a while, then we'll switch for a while."

She nodded, "Okay."

Joe patted me on the back and disappeared. The concert crowd seemed pretty calm, but with thousands of people talking, the noise was still pretty loud. Then the lights went out. Everything got quiet. Cheryl and I clung to each other. Suddenly the stage exploded with multi-colored lights and electric sound. The crowd went crazy as a hit song engulfed us.

Cheryl and I looked at each other and started kissing. What could be better than this? Our kiss lasted three or four songs. Suddenly Joe reappeared. He was a great friend, and if it wasn't for him we wouldn't have even been there, but I didn't think about anything except what I wanted. And at the moment I wanted to keep kissing Cheryl.

Have you ever felt that your own needs were more important than anyone else's? One way my brain injury affected me, as traumatic brain injuries tend to do, was to almost force me to focus on my own needs and wants. This limited my ability to care about others. I didn't purposely put other people's interests beneath mine; it's just that my own interests seemed so significant that it didn't even occur to me that other people had needs, too. I completely forgot that Joe had purchased the tickets for all of us and that he was a good friend. I forgot everything but my immediate wants. All I knew was that I had been enjoying kissing Cheryl and I wanted her to stay.

It's been twenty-one years, but I can still remember how I sat there without really listening to the music. I just sat there and pouted because Cheryl was gone. I still recall this incident because those same selfish concerns for my own needs at that time has cost me a number of friendships over the years. Friendships are like bank accounts. You can't take more out than you put in.

As time passed from my traumatic brain injury (TBI) until now, I gradually became aware of other people's needs. As this awareness grew, I had to consciously not criticize myself too severely for my earlier selfish behavior. Self-criticism helps no one, and it hurts the criticized.

Doing stand-up comedy in nightclubs and then progressing to delivering motivational talks for students in schools, elementary through university levels, helped me get my life going in a positive direction. The responsibility of speaking before audiences really helped improve my attitude and my ability to get along with people. With an improved attitude, life became a little smoother. And with a smoother life came an even better attitude. Right now my attitude is so good I can barely recognize myself.

How do you treat folks with physical or mental impairments? In my experience, people generally react to people with a TBI in one of three ways. People who have been around long enough to develop some compassion, tend to give people with a TBI the benefit of the doubt, which is welcome if it's done in a non-patronizing way. Other people are so ignorant that they either assume the physically apparent results of a TBI, like paralysis or speech impairment, are the only real consequences. And others assume that physical impairment means that the impaired person is as dumb as a post. Even though half my body was paralyzed and the TBI had interfered with my thinking and emotional processes, that didn't mean I was stupid.

It meant that my speed of thought was dramatically reduced and sometimes the conclusions I reached, especially involving emotional or interpersonal situations, were way off the mark. The wider the range of experiences a person has had, the larger that person's capacity is for dealing with people like me who may do or say things that are unexpected or inappropriate. My own ability to deal with folks who are not "normal" has grown drastically as a result of my having lived twenty-one years with a TBI. Because educating the entire public is unrealistic, people with a TBI must either adapt or move to a TBI commune.

With his stereo blasting so loudly I could hear him coming down the block, my friend Eric rolled up in his van and parked in my driveway. The Eric Clapton concert didn't begin for another couple hours, so we had plenty of time. I came out on the porch as Eric rolled down his window and shouted, "Let's go, Dude. It'll take an hour to get down there, plus we've still gotta get some beer."

Gripping my cane, I hobbled out to his van. Joe had moved back to New Jersey, and I'd begun going to concerts with a new friend named Eric Robson. A few years older than I am, he's been a guitarist in rock bands for years before becoming lead guitarist with "Solar Wind," a popular jazz band.

My friendship with Eric has lasted for more than a decade because he understands people's differences. He knows that some people don't always fit our expectations. Learning to accept people, without expecting them to be any certain way, has been one of the most valuable lessons I've learned from Eric and from my own experiences with TBI folks and people in general.

Making friends is much easier since I learned two important things. The importance of not taking more out of a relationship than I'm willing to put in, and the importance of accepting people exactly as they are.

Chapter 6
Blaming Circumstances: "It's Not My Fault"

"There is luxury in self-reproach. When we blame ourselves we feel that no one else has a right to blame us. It is the confession, not the priest that gives us absolution."
—Oscar Wilde

What was it like for you?" Cindy asked as she turned her wheelchair toward me. Because I'm fairly outgoing and because I like to hear other perspectives, I'll frequently talk with people in wheelchairs or those who look like they've had a rough time. When I saw Cindy's wheelchair at a table outside a coffee café, I went over and started talking with her.

"Wow," I said, after hearing Cindy's description of what she saw while she was in her coma. Apparently she had witnessed a dark tunnel and a bright light.

"I knew the light was total love," she said. "Tell me what your coma was like."

I shrugged. I was tempted to make up some kind of fantastic story about bright lights, dark tunnels, and angels, but it seemed kind of silly. Many people have asked if I have any memory of the time I was in a coma. They go on to describe different out-of-body, near death experiences they either had or heard of someone else having while comatose.

If it is possible to have such an experience, I wish I'd had one. That way I would be more inclined to believe folks who say they did. But I didn't, so I don't. Okay, so I'm a cynic. Sue me.

One year after my accident, Cheryl left me. With my cane lying on the floor beside the recliner, I slouched into the overstuffed chair staring at the TV, but I saw nothing. What would happen to me? Would I ever get married? Would I ever have another girlfriend as pretty as Cheryl? Would I ever have another good job? Would I ever have any of the things I'd once had or do any of the things I once did? I'd been on top of the world, now I was in the pit of hell. My pet terrier sat on the floor beside me. I patted his head. Why couldn't I have been a dog?

Cheryl and I had started attending church a few weeks before my accident. I thought I was making God happy, but apparently not. Who is God? Who knows what God wants? God is different to different people. But no matter whether a person thinks God is a light bulb or a doorknob or a pinecone, I think times of trouble are times when most people turn to their idea of God and ask for help. But, because my accident coincided with when I started going to church, I was torn. Half of me wanted to ask for help, but the other half of me remembered what had happened last time I had showed an interest in spiritual things.

Thick gray clouds and cool autumn air made this a typical October Sunday. I was hobbling around the block. Many times in the first ten years of recovery, I asked God "Why did You let this happen? And if it was You who let it happen, why did You have to wake me up from my coma? And if it was You who woke me up, why didn't You wake me up all the way? Why did You have to leave half my body paralyzed?"

I kept hobbling along with my cane held off the ground. I staggered to a stop, planted my cane on the ground to keep my balance then looked up at the sky. "Come on, answer me! Why did You do it? Health, possessions, relationships, I had everything I wanted. Then I went back to church and now I've got nothing. Why?" I spit on the sidewalk. Who am I talking to? Next I'll be seeing bright lights and dark tunnels.

"If You're up there, or out there, You should've let me die!"

Because I had based my happiness on my circumstances, until I accepted my new circumstances, I felt no joy. When I say "accept my circumstances," I'm not saying that I quit wishing I was whole or that I quit doing everything I could to get back as many of my physical capabilities as possible—not at all. Accepting what had happened to me didn't give me an excuse to not do my best to become everything I could. Just the opposite! When I finally accepted what had happened to me, I quit being angry over what happened and I quit being full of self-pity. I began seeing my new limitations as challenges that could be either overcome or dealt with.

Accepting myself as a person with a disability means accepting my limitations and it also means accepting responsibility for making the most of the abilities I still have. For example, I still have a sense of humor and I still love to write. Although I can no longer be productive at a job requiring physical strength and dexterity or quick decision making, there are certain things I can still do. For me, accepting my disability includes changing my outlook and my occupation and becoming productive in a new way.

Until I finally accepted myself as a person with different strengths from the ones I had before, my attitude made me so hard to deal with people frequently chose not to be around me. For years I thought other people's perception of my disability was my biggest handicap, but now I can see that my negative attitude was the bigger handicap. In the long run, and sometimes even in the short run, my attitude is more important than my physical attributes. My attitude determines people's perception of my disability.

Partly because of fear that they will make a bad situation even worse and partially because they just don't care to deal with a potentially awkward situation, folks tend to shy away from people with disabilities. And, if the person with a disability also has a negative attitude, people don't just shy away, they run away.

Of course they run away. We all have stuff we'd rather not deal with. The last thing any sane person wants is to spend time with someone who wastes time brooding about his troubles, which is why I used spend a lot of time alone. I was hungry for companionship, but I was a miserable companion. I was a living paradox. Since I wanted friends, I tried to pull people into my life. My friendly approach invited them in, but my negative attitude pushed them back out.

Before acceptance came, I had it in my head that if I just tried hard enough, I'd be able to make my life just as it was before. With that in mind, I lunged after my goals of talking, walking, and driving like a wild gorilla might lunge after a run-away banana cart. Instead of having the peace that eventually came with acceptance, I had a constant feeling of alienation and desperation.

I was desperate to recapture the life I had had, but my negative attitude alienated potential friends. Accepting my situation freed me from the ball-and-chain-negative-attitude I had been dragging around. And once the chain broke, I was free to focus on goals that would make the most out of what I had left.

My primary goals of talking, walking, and driving a car excited my imagination. But in the beginning, they were too far out of reach to waste time focusing on. Luckily, I had a whole string of smaller goals, like not drooling out of the paralyzed side of my mouth, tying my shoe-laces with one hand, and controlling my bladder till I reached the bathroom so I could quit wearing a catheter. These goals sound minor, but each goal I reached contributed to raising my self-esteem. And the way I feel about myself has everything to do with how I feel about people and what I choose to accomplish.

One of my earliest goals was to go to college and become an accountant. How I came up with the idea of being an accountant is a mystery to me. It's a good choice for someone with a healthy brain who also enjoys tedious, repetitive work. Someone like me taking accounting was like trying to teach a baboon to play chess. Not only did it take me an absurdly long time to understand new concepts, I couldn't concentrate for more than a few minutes at a time. But I had one vital ingredient.

I had tenacity! And I had all the time in the world. To make a long story shorter, I'll just tell you I never did manage to pound the accounting principals into my brain. But, since I had started college and since I had nothing else to do, I was determined to finish it. Luckily, I was going to a two-year college.

I began college a year and a half after my injury. Although academics were my apparent reason for going, my real focus was learning to function without being angry and bitter, or ashamed of what I'd become.

The day before the first day of class, I went to speak with the teacher. She called me into her office.

"You wanted to see me?"

"Yes."

Suddenly I felt very stupid. Maybe this wasn't such a great idea after all. But I was afraid what would happen if I didn't do it. She was looking at me. I cleared my throat.

"Mrs. (I forgot her name), my speech impairment makes people think I'm retarded. I was wondering if, on the first day of class, it'd be okay if I told everybody why I talk the way I do."

She looked about my mom's age. She might have had kids about my age. Her expression said she understood what I was feeling.

"You don't need to," she said. "But if it's something you want to do, you can."

My embarrassment over my speech impairment was pretty severe, but it never kept me from speaking my mind. College students seemed to be less preoccupied with my speech impairment than most people in the general public, and after that first class, I quit feeling a need to explain myself.

In fact, being treated well by college students was the first in a series of experiences that gave me confidence to expect the same from other people, and this confidence took away a lot of the intimidation I felt around groups of noisy, laughing, talking people. Trying to interact with a lot of people at once is still frustrating and difficult, but now I'm confident enough to do it with an ever-increasing level of success.

In order to enjoy mingling in crowds, my expectations had to change. The same rules for one-to-one courtesy and thoughtfulness apply, but since I don't speak or think as quickly and clearly as I used to, I had to learn to hold my tongue instead of just jumping into the flow of conversation. When I did jump in, things usually ground to a halt until people could figure out what I was talking about. Either that or my quiet monotone voice went unnoticed. I didn't enjoy either of these, so I gradually learned to avoid trying to be the center of attention. It's not that I killed the urge; I still like to be the center of attention. That is what gave me the drive to become a professional comedian. As a comedian, not only am I the only one in the room with a microphone, people actually pay to hear what I have to say.

What's even funnier is that I'm also paid to talk in schools. Did you hear me? When I was growing up, teachers would have liked to kick me out for talking in school. Now they call and offer me money to talk in school. Is that cool or what?

Anyway, seven years after starting school at a community college, I walked down the aisle and finally got my diploma. WINNERS Don't Quit! Winners DON'T Quit!! Winners Don't QUIT!!!

I made one more try at a four-year school before having to face the fact that regular college was out of reach. Oh well, I gave it a shot. Because accounting had given me so much trouble the first time, I decided to take a six-month accounting course. Man was that tough! I hated it. But I stuck it out and got an "A." One valuable thing I learned from studying accounting was that I will never settle for a job as tedious as bookkeeping. My accountant has a very nice income, but I would never want to have to do what he does. All those numbers and legal forms and tax books and the list goes on.

My webmaster is another important person in my life who's got a job I wouldn't want. He's great at high tech computer mumbo jumbo and he seems to love it, but leave me out of it. Just send me the bill.

Thankfully, different people have different gifts. And no matter what gifts we have, I still believe the most valuable skill anyone can have is the ability to get along well with people!

Chapter 7

Triumph on the Highway

Imagination is more important than knowledge.
—Albert Einstein

Have you ever wanted something—really wanted it—and everybody said you'd never get it? One thing I really wanted during my rehabilitation was to be able to drive again. I had to get my driver's license back. But when I asked a doctor at Harborview, he told me flat out, "Al, you'll never drive again."

So the next day, I went to the driver's retraining program at the University of Washington Hospital, and they told me the same thing. They wouldn't even let me into their program. I was furious! These guys were getting paid to help folks rehabilitate, but were they? No! Mad as I was, I was more determined than ever to get my driver's license back.

But how could I? They all said I'd never drive again.

I angrily gripped my cane and hobbled back to the bus stop. I slumped in the bus seat and tried to think of something else I could do to get back my license, but I'd tried everything I could think of. Except … but would he?

Luckily, good old dad came to the rescue. My father and I had been buddies since I was born. We had skied and backpacked together, and he wanted to see me get my game back. Not only that, his own father had suffered a head injury similar to mine in the First

World War. I think he knew that my angry verbal outbursts would not become physical.

Like I said, I think he knew. Maybe he didn't. Anyway, my dad borrowed a neighbor's beat up Oldsmobile, he handed me the keys, and we went out driving. I drove all the back roads in western Washington between Everett and Renton and between Redmond and Duvall.

One day as I was leaving Redmond, red lights flashed behind me, and a siren wailed. Oh no! I pulled over to the side of the road and looked in my rear view mirror just in time to see a cop climb out of his car. He stood there for a good minute. I'm not sure, but he might have been brushing powdered sugar and donut crumbs off his shirt, before he came marching up to my car.

"You been drinking young man?"

"No. The reason I …" When he heard my bark, the cop's eyes popped open so wide, his sunglasses almost fell off. When my dad explained what was going on—the officer was very supportive. After wishing us good luck, he sent us on our way.

About this time, I received my first small payment from the insurance company of the guy whose truck I had crashed into when he ran the stop sign. I used the money to buy a customized Datsun pick-up. It was a black flatbed with dual gold wheels, oak side rails, a lockable wood tool box, smoke stacks, and the words "Born to Run"—after Bruce Springsteen's then popular album—painted on each door.

The hospital elevator had never seemed so slow. It stopped on every floor. People got on and off, some asking directions and then standing there looking confused. Finally we reached the fourth floor. I staggered out and stumbled down the hall.

Knock, knock, knock.

"Come in."

I pushed the door open, hobbled in and plopped onto a chair looking at my psychologist.

"Doc, do you think I'll ever get my driver's license back?"

"Al, we've been over this and over this. You will never drive again."

I'll never forget the feelings of pride in my chest and the psychologist's stunned expression when I pulled out my new driver's license and waved it in his face. My speech therapist was right: WINNERS Don't Quit! Winners DON'T Quit!! Winners Don't QUIT!!! There are no limits!

Chapter 8

To Live or Not To Live

Suicide is man's way of telling God, "You can't fire me—I quit.
—Bill Maher, 1995 on Politically Incorrect

What is more powerful than your choices? Nothing! Rehabilitation has been a series of choices: choosing to go to therapy, choosing to exercise between sessions, choosing to follow the advice of therapists, and choosing to look on the bright side when everything seemed dark. Things seemed so dark and desperate at times that I wished I were dead. It's a good thing I was too chicken to commit suicide.

The process of rehabilitation brings about more than physical changes. It's also a process of going from a point of feeling worthless to a point of feeling like I'm on top of my game. It has been a twenty-one-year journey for me, and it's not over yet. I still have plenty of goals, but I've also achieved plenty. Reaching those goals and getting regular exercise makes me feel so good about who I am that I know reaching my other goals is only a matter of time.

One of the most profound lessons rehabilitation has taught me is that I choose the way I feel. For example, if I choose to talk a certain way, I will feel the way I talk. If I say negative things, I feel negative, but if I speak positively, I feel positive. I don't speak how I feel as often as I feel how I speak.

Six or seven years after my injury, the insurance company quit paying for therapy. By then I knew everything the therapist was going to have me do anyway so when a colorful newspaper ad for a local health club caught my eye, I read the whole thing. I'd belonged to the YMCA for years, but never to one of the fancier health clubs. The ad offered huge savings and pictured some great equipment the Y had never had. I used a cane, so it was evident, at least to me, that I still needed therapy. But why should I pay for it when I already knew what the therapist was going to have me do? Why not spend the money that therapy would have cost on a place with nicer equipment?

Treadmills and three different kinds of stair climbing machines filled one room. The cool breeze coming from the fans washed over my back. Since I couldn't run, I put the treadmill on the steepest grade possible and, gripping the bar beside the track, I hobbled along. I felt like a disabled gerbil running on its little wheel.

After the treadmill, I tried the nautilus equipment. Facing the huge wall mirrors around the exercise room, the chest press quickly became my favorite. Push, ease up. Push, ease up. Push, ease up. Adrenaline flowed through my veins. Straining the non-paralyzed muscles on my right side got my endorphins pumping and lifted my spirits so high that one night I dreamed about joining the Para-Olympics (Olympics for people with disabilities).

The dream began with me standing among a group of people with disabilities ranging from amputations to head injuries. The first event I was in was the boxing competition. My first opponent was a blind guy. He looked pretty tough, but I knew I could beat him. I had only one problem. Every time I got close to him, his dog bit me. If I'd been thinking like a non-brain damaged person, I would have distracted the dog with a milk bone, and knocked the blind guy out. But by the time I thought of this, the match was over. That's why they're called the Para-Olympics.

I can hear some politically correct activist saying, "That's not right! He shouldn't be talking about beating up blind guys."

Relax. It was a dream.

I've come to learn that perhaps the greatest power anyone can have is the power of choice. How we choose to see life and limits is up to us. Do I choose to see challenges or calamities? Am I a winner or a loser? For years, I didn't realize how much power I had. All I knew was I was miserable and no change was in sight. I thought my only choice was to continue suffering, or throw in my cards and finally have peace.

I'd been toying with this idea ever since I came out of my coma, but I never really planned to do it. But no matter how hard I worked, things didn't get better. A long dark tunnel stretched out before me, with no light at the other end. I was like a tiny ant looking up a slippery sewer pipe, knowing there was no other way out.

After my fiancée Cheryl left me, the combination of losing her, losing other relationships, losing the material things I had—and worse—losing my ability to get them back, pushed me over the edge.

Once I made the decision, I had a sense of peace. Being able to check out gave me a feeling of power. Think how nice it would be to not have to face life with only half a body. Think how nice it would be to not have to try to function with a sluggish, forgetful, erratically undependable brain and severely unstable emotions.

Sometimes my brain would erupt with so many different ideas that while trying to figure out which one to say next, I'd forget half of what I had started to say, so my words would just peter out. Even though I had complete ideas, by the time I tried to say them, I forgot what they were. To make matters worse, my reflexes were so slow that, sometimes, by the time I verbalized my thoughts, whoever I was talking to had already changed subjects two or three times.

When my fiancée, who had been my constant companion since my accident, told me our relationship was over, my worst fears came to life. How would I deal with life alone? Of course, I still had my family, thank God. But I was hungry for something a family couldn't give.

Coincidentally, at this same time, another attractive blonde who knew the family my fiancée had been staying with, came to town to stay with them for a while. She was going through a nasty divorce. We hooked up. She was broken up about her divorce and I was broken up about losing Cheryl. At the time, it sounded like a match made in heaven. And it was … for a few weeks. But it ended in a ball of flames and burnt ashes. I went back to the choice I'd already made.

The morning sun streamed through my bedroom window promising another beautiful day. I pulled on my clothes and went down to breakfast. After eating, I went out to my flatbed Datsun. It only took a few minutes to drive to the freeway overpass. I parked off the road. I took out my cane and hobbled onto the bridge.

I walked like a condemned man. My heart weighed a ton. What was I doing? This had seemed like a good idea at first, but the closer I got to actually doing it, the more the permanence of this solution gave me pause. I wasn't ready to back out entirely, though. I just had to stop and think it over. I stopped in the middle of the overpass, staring down at the cars passing underneath. I don't know how long I stood there or how long she'd been watching me, but suddenly a soft female voice broke into my thoughts.

"Hi."

"Huh?" I glanced behind me. An attractive young lady stood there.

"Do you want to talk?" I didn't say anything.

"What's wrong?" she asked.

What's wrong? Boy did I have an earful for her. It was as if someone pushed the cork into an upside down wine bottle. All the wine wanted to come out, but the cork, lodged in the bottle's neck, kept the wine from flowing freely. It just dribbled out. All my woes wanted to come pouring out, but how could I explain how it felt going from the top of the world to the pit of hell?

She must have sensed my confusion and desperation. She raised her hand, motioning to a car down the street.

A patrol car drove up and stopped by the curb beside us. The attractive woman was an undercover cop. They took me to the psychiatric ward at Overlake Hospital in Bellevue, Washington. Wow! Three days in that place opened my eyes. Having my perception adjusted did me a world of good. Sure, my situation might not be ideal, but I was a lot better off than a lot of the folks in the psych ward. I was reminded that life isn't always a bowl of good times and happy feelings. I realized that some people saw an even more dismal view of the world than I did. It's amazing how much this did to put everything in perspective. In other words, all I had to do was open my eyes. Like the old saying goes, "Wake up and smell the coffee, Waldo!"

Chapter 9
Facing Life on My Own

A man has to live with himself,
and he should see to it that he always has good company.
—Charles Evans Hughes

As I sat at a picnic table on the grass by the beach on Kirkland's waterfront eating an ice cream cone, Erica's dog perked up its ears and politely eyed the remaining couple bites of the cone. The Kirkland waterfront is a favorite hangout in spring and summer for young and old, male and female, married and single—mostly single.

When Erica saw the little Bible on the bench beside me, her eyes lit up.

"Are you a Christian, too?"

"Not really," I shrugged. "I just read the Bible 'cause I like the way it makes me feel."

"Really? Have you ever been to the So-and-So singles?"

I shook my head, "No."

Erica explained that the group was a gathering of single folks about my age who met once a week and did things together. She told me where they met, and I said I'd check them out.

I've been hanging out with this group for a long time now. While school helped me a little to interact with folks as a person with new limitations, I found the schoolwork distracting. The singles group allows me to interact with folks without having to worry about doing homework.

Regaining my driver's license made me redouble my efforts to walk without a cane. I thought that if I learned to walk and talk better, life would return to the way it had been before my accident. I couldn't have been more wrong. My life would never be the same. I wasn't happy until I accepted my new life and limitations, and quit trying to recapture the old. Working hard is fine, but wasting time and energy trying to regain something that's gone forever is not only discouraging, it's just plain stupid.

For some reason, I got it in my head that living with my parents was holding me back. I couldn't have been more wrong. Anyway, I got a newspaper and turned to the "Wanted to Share" section of the classified ads. Most of the places I called hung up as soon as they heard my speech impairment. They didn't even give me long enough to explain why I talked the way I did. This hurt my feelings and made me super mad. It also embarrassed me so much that when my dad asked about the brevity of one such call, I told him I had called a wrong number. I vowed more than once that I'd call back and harass people who hung up because of my speech impairment. But I always managed to simmer down before I did it.

Writing this reminds me that I worked for several months as a telemarketer with American Handicapped Workers. Telemarketing was tough, but asking people to buy light bulbs proved easier than asking people if I could live with them. Actually, sounding like I was handicapped probably helped me sell a few more light bulbs.

Finally I found a place to live. It was an older five-bedroom house shared by five people. I was the fifth. My desire to walk without a cane really took shape and became an overpowering goal. I'd hold my cane off the ground and stagger down the sidewalk until I lost my balance, then I'd plant my cane to keep from falling. I didn't always plant it quickly enough. I fell a lot. Once I hit my face on the sidewalk and had to get four stitches.

I also started drinking about this time. I didn't drink for the first year after my accident, because I'd been told that drinking while taking anti-seizure medication could result in a continuing series of seizures, which would ensure that I'd never be able to drive. But that concern was over. I was off the medication and I was driving, so I started drinking. The problem was that alcohol and depression go together like poor dental hygiene and cavities. The more I drank, the more depressed I got. I wasn't a daily drinker. I only drank every few days, but when I drank, I drank a lot.

Actually, I wasn't drinking as much as the four others in the house, but they were older than me and had more years of practice consuming alcohol. Plus, neither my body nor my emotions were functioning at an optimal level—even when I wasn't drunk. To make a long and somewhat embarrassing story short, I'll just say that I was asked to move on down the road. Their distinct message was that I vacate the premises so quickly that the screen door didn't hit my backside on the way out.

I never drank while I was practicing walking, I didn't have to. I walked like I was drunk without drinking. One day a red-faced man with a beer belly yelled off his porch. "Hey, guy. You're too drunk to walk. You need a designated walker."

Yeah, whatever.

Exercise was and still is a daily thing for me. I enjoy walking, but I enjoy even more exercising on the health club's exercise machines. You can't even tell I'm paralyzed when I'm sitting at one of these machines. People line up behind me to use it when I'm done. You should see how quickly they lose interest when I get up and hobble away. "I'm not using that machine. Look what it did to him."

I really like the swimming pool. I'm out there doing the one-handed overhand crawl. I meet lots of people since I'm always swimming in circles.

Over the years I began using my cane less and less, walking and limping along for greater and greater distances without it. By 1996, I was walking without it more frequently than I was using it. Today, twenty-one years after my injury, I never use it in the city, but I keep it around for outdoor hikes. I get together with friends just about every week and hike through different areas of woods where the trails can get rough.

Chapter 10

Fast Cars and Bad Attitudes

The greatest discovery of my generation is that a human being can alter his life by altering his attitudes of mind.
—William James

When I moved out on my own, my disability check was all I had for income. I soon discovered that the kind of folks I could afford to call neighbors were not exactly upper middle class professionals. You know—overgrown lawns, broken sidewalks, older houses with peeling paint, and down the block, an old Chevy Impala with one flat tire sat by the curb.

Maybe I should've kept living with my parents.

My neighbors, however, were not my biggest problem. I was. I realize now that people avoided me because of my negative attitude. I liked people and wanted friendships, but my negativity and self-pity chased them away. The kind of people who hung around me felt as bad about themselves as I felt about myself. I dealt with my negative attitude and growing depression by getting real drunk every few days.

The problem with trying to cure depression by drinking was that drinking made me more depressed. And, without even realizing I was doing it, I'd look for reasons to justify my depression. I found them, too. At the top of my list of reasons to be depressed was that my fiancée had left me. That really stung! Whenever I got drunk or whenever anything happened to remind me of losing her—and it's amazing how easily I was reminded—I dove into a state of depression.

Being in a depressed and drunken state one day, I staggered out of my house to get into my car. Even with a cane, my walking was so erratic that a neighbor lady saw me stumbling along and hurried over to try to prevent me from driving off. We talked for a few minutes and then suddenly a patrol car pulled up. I realized she'd called the cops before coming out.

She grabbed my keys and ran back to the police car. I took out my spare key and drove off. The cops turned on their siren and began the chase. My heart raced. My depression was gone. This was fun. My house was two blocks from Interstate 5. I don't know what I was thinking, but luckily I headed for the freeway—lucky because I was too drunk to go racing around narrow back streets.

Once on I-5, the race was quickly over, so I stopped. I figured they might be a bit upset, but I had no idea they'd be furious. Until that day, I had dealt with courteous cops who politely handed me another ticket. There was nothing courteous about those two cops. They stormed up to my car, and even before I could tell them that I was half paralyzed, that I was head injured, and that I was sorry, they yanked me out of my car and pushed me face down onto the street. They handcuffed me and carted me off to jail!

As I crouched in the back of the patrol car during the ride in, I did some serious thinking. My depression was over. I had to think of a way to avoid getting a DWI? By the time we got to the police station, I had it all worked out.

It's been many years since that day, so my recollection of the exact conversation is a bit fuzzy, but I was brought into a room where they fingerprinted me and asked some questions. That was when I put my anti-DWI plan into effect. I didn't look forward to going into another psychiatric hospital, but it sure beat getting a DWI. Come to think of it, I didn't even get a speeding ticket that day.

It took me a long time to clear my head and improve my outlook and thereby my circumstances. As long as I was getting drunk, things didn't change. Having alcohol flow through my system impaired my thinking and held me back. Another thing that held me back was the way I spoke.

Because I hated my injury, I spoke like I hated it. I was angry and I sounded angry. I saw problems everywhere I looked. The whole world was lined up waiting to take advantage of me. Thinking and speaking this way made me see things in the most negative light possible. Because I was drowning in negativity, every time I opened my mouth, I spit out insults, profanity, and criticism. It was a vicious circle.

One day I got sick and tired of the rut I was in. I had already attempted suicide and chickened out, so I felt stuck. Was there anything else I could do? I decided to call my mom. She would know what I should do. I didn't explain to her all the trouble I'd been in. I didn't want to cause her any alarm and cloud the issue.

Her suggestion was one I would never have thought of: "Why don't you go to Walla Walla College where your brother is going?" It was summer, so the next fall I transferred from a community college to WWC. Wow! What a great, positive experience. Although the positive atmosphere did me a world of good, my academic wheels were spinning like car tires on ice. Walla Walla College is a great school for people without brain damage.

At least being in a very positive environment, I was able to free myself from the bottle. I began finishing classes!

But alcohol is cunning and powerful, and by the third quarter, I was beginning to drink again. Just a little in the evening at first. But then I started drinking at lunchtime, then before class, and pretty soon I was going to class drunk. Before I knew it, I was almost as bad off as before going to WWC. Thankfully, faculty at WWC was more concerned about my welfare than the faculty at the community college.

I was told that I couldn't re-enroll until I returned to Seattle and completed an inpatient alcohol treatment program. I took their advice, completed the program, and when I re-enrolled at WWC, I was clean and sober. I thought I'd do better at my studies now that I had stopped drinking. But other difficulties emerged because I'd already taken the easier classes, and the remaining ones were a lot tougher—classes like World History. That class was my undoing. The required reading was drudgery, but I hung in there and finished every page.

Things would have been fine except that besides reading about world history, I was also expected to understand and remember what I'd read. Yeah right. Like a crammed hard drive, my brain was reaching its maximum capacity just doing the reading. Trying to actually understand and recall what I read was too much. So I called it quits and finished up earning a two-year degree at a community college in Seattle.

In 1995, fifteen years after my accident, I again tried a four-year school: Western Washington University. Unfortunately, all that did was reconfirm my limitations. Brain damage still held me in its grasp. I was not capable of learning and then applying what I'd learned to hold down a job. Looking back, the most important lesson college taught me was the value of getting along well with people. But re-learning this lesson was tricky.

As a teenager, I had always gotten along well with people. But trying to relate normally to people now was a real challenge. With a ruptured hypothalamus, shattered memory, slow understanding, and a state of depression—you begin to understand what I was up against.

If it hadn't been for one major change in my outlook, things would still be the same. I would have continued seeing calamities instead of challenges. I would have continued to be a depressed fountain of negativity. Then, through a string of insights and realizations, my outlook changed. I began to see possibilities instead of limitations. And one key realization allowed me to change my perceptions and change my life.

Chapter 11

The Power of Words

The words 'I am' are potent words; be careful what you hitch them to. The thing you're claiming has a way of reaching back and claiming you.
—A. L. Kitselman

Do you like being on stage? Are we ever really off stage?

The stage lights hid the audience, but I knew they were there. I held the microphone the magician handed me and spoke into it.

"Wow! Was he hot or what? Where'd those cards come from?"

The audience applauded wildly as he made his way off stage. The magic man had seemed to "speak" cards, as well as coke bottles and bananas into and out of existence. In a way, his act was a lot like life. We're all magicians, but only a few of us realize the magical powers we have.

It's amazing to me that I took so long to see the correlation between what I said and what happened to me. I was like a magician—the more I said negative things, the more anger and depression popped out of the hat. When I finally became aware of this, I spoke with my psychologist about it, and I started reading books on the subject.

I gradually realized that I had made a life-changing discovery. I had discovered that my words—anyone's words—are like magic. Our words have the power to tear us down or build us up. Our words can tear others down or build them up. Whether we see ourselves as winners or losers determines how we talk. And how we talk determines whether we are winners or losers.

Winners can afford to build people up. Losers, to feel better about themselves, spend their time tearing others down. The problem with tearing people down to build yourself up is that you begin to feel contempt for yourself. The beauty of this truth is that its opposite is also true. When you say and do things to build people up—when you smile, listen, encourage, recognize, and sincerely appreciate others—you feel worthwhile yourself.

In other words, we can choose whether we want to be a winner or a loser.

Being a winner or a loser determines how we choose to see our life's circumstances. Do we choose to see obstacles or opportunities? Do we choose to speak about our victories or our failures? It's our choice.

Changing from speaking like a loser to speaking like a winner took me a long time for two reasons. One reason was the company I kept. I hung around people who spoke negatively. The second reason was because the negative words I kept speaking made me think negatively. Our words have incredible power on us and on others.

Some people believe that you speak the way you feel. That's only half-correct. How we feel is as much a result of how we speak, as how we speak is a result of how we feel. Sounds circular, right? That's because it is. I know from my experience and that of others, that we don't speak the way we feel as often as we feel the way we speak. The next time you feel low, try saying only cheerful, positive things to folks. You will soon begin feeling better. As the old saying goes: "Fake it 'till you make it."

An image I use in some of my talks is this. I picture each person having an imaginary bucket inside of himself. The bucket holds that person's self-esteem and level of confidence. Each time I do or say something that hurts this person, I punch a hole in that person's self-esteem bucket. At the same time, I puncture my own bucket. Every time I do something to help the person fill his or her bucket, I fill my own bucket with increased self-esteem.

Following my accident, one of my greatest needs was to rebuild my confidence. My poor self-image contributed to my social problems. I began asking psychologists how to feel better about myself, and I paid particular attention to things that filled my self-esteem bucket. If each of us realized how much our self-esteem bucket fills up when we fill other people's buckets, there would be bucket brigades everywhere.

In the next chapter, I'll describe what I discovered about filling my self-esteem bucket to overflowing.

Chapter 12

Filling Your Self-Esteem Bucket

In my day, we didn't have self-esteem, we had self-respect, and no more of it than we had earned.
—Jane Haddam

As soon as I opened my mouth and asked the woman behind the grocery store's cash register how much a Snickers bar cost, I could tell from her expression that there would be a problem.

"Pardon me?" she said.

I repeated myself, very carefully enunciating each word. She understood me; she must have. She repeated her answer back to me, slowly and loudly enough for everybody in the store to hear. She said, f-i-f-t-e-e-n c-e-n-t-s.

I scowled and loudly said, "T—h—a—n—k y—o—u."

It got a few laughs, but episodes like this drained my self-esteem. Why did that cashier have to embarrass me? Why did I have to react? My actions had brought more attention to the embarrassing situation than hers had.

Every now and then I did receive a dose of encouragement. The family my fiancée had lived with was always supportive, perhaps because the husband had suffered a head-injury years before.

"You've done so well, Al. Your parents must be awfully proud of you," the wife would say. She was always saying positive things to me.

I'd shrug, "Yeah. They're proud. Who can blame 'em?"

I laughed and made little jokes whenever people complimented me. It was hard for me to accept compliments because I couldn't believe they were sincere. I thought people said nice things to me because they felt sorry for me. During the initial years after my accident, people complimented me and frequently told me they admired all the hard work I was doing. This would have boosted my self-esteem, if only I had believed them. But how could I believe them? I saw myself as pathetic, someone to be pitied, not someone who deserved respect or admiration.

As I mentioned, during this time if I received a positive compliment, I'd laugh and shrug it off. However, when someone said something negative or derogatory about me, I latched onto it and made it part of my self-belief. This was something I could identify with because it was what I already believed about myself.

In other words, all my accomplishments, all the goals I reached, and limits I overcame did not fill my self-esteem bucket because of the negative way I thought and spoke about myself. Speaking positively, to myself and others, is the most important thing I can do to raise my self-esteem. Here are eight powerful steps I've discovered for filling your bucket with self-esteem and genuine confidence.

1. Appreciate myself

I appreciate myself for the goals I've achieved. And if I can't achieve an entire goal, I celebrate the part I did achieve. For example, one of my goals was to run again. Am I running? No. But at least I no longer have to use a walker or a cane. Another goal was to sing. Am I singing? No. But do I have to point out letters on an alphabet board? No I don't.

It was also my goal to be a good driver. Am I a good driver? No. But at least I don't have to take the bus or rely on others to shuttle me around. The point is that the harder I try to reach a goal, the more my self-esteem bucket is filled, even if I don't reach the goal completely. If I reach every goal the first time I try, my goals are too easy. I add the most to my self-esteem bucket by trying and failing and trying again until I succeed. Then I take a little time to celebrate my victories.

2. Keep my promises

If I promise myself I'll get up early and go walking, or get up early and do whatever, then I do it. Breaking promises pokes holes in my self-esteem bucket. Keeping promises fills my bucket.

3. Exercise often

Physical exercise not only affects a body's chemical balance and keeps it healthier, it increases the flow of oxygen to every cell in the body and releases chemical endorphins that make me feel better about myself.

4. Read daily

"I took a speed reading course and read 'War and Peace' in twenty minutes. It involves Russia." —Woody Allen

Apparently I thought that was funny. But reading is great mental exercise and with brain damage I need all the help I can get.

5. Appreciate others

"Appreciation is a wonderful thing: It makes what is excellent in others belong to us as well." —Voltaire

Remember how good you feel when you do something for others that makes them feel good about themselves? The most reliable way to fill your own self-esteem bucket is to help others fill theirs. Listening wholeheartedly to others, sincerely complimenting them, keeping a promise, giving a ride, or solving problems for others are ways to help fill their self-esteem bucket.

On the other hand, lying to people, insulting them, taking things from them, or gossiping are ways to empty their buckets—and yours.

I know a remarkable woman who's a professional comedian named Debbie who, as a single parent with polio and with no help from her ex-husband, raised five kids to be law-abiding, respectable citizens. Debbie clearly understood the self-esteem-bucket concept. Whenever one of her kids did something to poke a hole in a sibling's bucket, she made the offender plug the hole by apologizing and then refill the bucket with compliments. She made the offender go off and write five things he or she liked about the brother or sister and then come back and read the list to that person out loud.

6. Think positively

Imagine positive things. The mind always tries to complete or accomplish whatever it pictures, so picture positive things. If you say you're going to fail, or you say you're going to succeed, you're mind will do its best to complete the picture. In other words, visualize success.

If you are a religious person, there's plenty of evidence indicating that God is trustworthy, so place your trust in Christ, God, or whichever Supreme Being you believe in. If you don't believe in anyone or anything but yourself, then why are you reading my book or anyone's? Why don't you write your own?

7. Don't quit

Remember that failing is part of succeeding. Overcoming failures builds confidence. Filling your self-esteem bucket involves failing. Try. Fail. Get up and keep trying until you succeed.

8. Treasure friends

One thing I've learned about friendships is that friendships are like bank accounts—you can't maintain a friendship by taking out more than you put in. I continually work at building and maintaining friendships. E-mail is a great way to keep in touch.

With these eight self-esteem building tools, you too can set out to fill your self-esteem bucket. Being born rich, talented, or beautiful is not nearly as important as deciding what to do with what you've been given. To have the best, be your best. There are no limits to being a caring and forgiving person.

Chapter 13

The Company We Keep

Without friends no one would choose to live,
though he had all other goods.
—Aristotle

How much are you influenced by the people around you?

When comedy club audiences laugh at a joke, I keep it. If they don't laugh, I either change it until they do laugh, or I quit using it. I'm not the only one who's influenced by other people. We all are.

Not only are we influenced by others, we imitate them. When I want to acquire a particular ability or habit, I hang around with folks who already have the habit, or with others who also want to develop it. What I see my associates doing has a profound effect on what I do.

If a thirty-second commercial can sell us a product, doesn't it stand to reason that the people we choose to work with and spend time with can sell us a lifestyle? Doesn't it also stand to reason that the type of shows we watch on TV or the type of music we listen to can influence our values?

Remember the mythical three monkeys? One monkey has his eyes covered, another his mouth covered, the third his ears covered. Below the monkey figurines are signs that read: see no evil, hear no evil, and speak no evil. Those monkeys were geniuses!

Life is fun, but it's also serious. There are no practice runs. There are no directors running around saying "Take 2", "Take 3." No! You get one shot and that's it. Since my choices are so powerful, I don't waste my time with negative folks who influence me to act negatively. That's my choice.

I began developing this attitude one afternoon. I had just completed my third trip around the block. My roommate John was sitting on the front porch.

"Why do you do all that walking?" John asked.

He was approaching middle age. He had been a Jesuit priest before he lost the vision he said God had given him.

I plopped in a chair beside him.

"What a stupid question," I said.

"Maybe it is, but the answer doesn't have to be stupid."

I looked at him. "What do you mean?"

"Think about the question. Why do you walk so much?"

"So someday I can walk without this stupid cane."

"Do you see yourself walking without a cane?"

"Of course!"

"Then you probably will. We become the way we see ourselves."

I sighed and shrugged. Sometimes John got too heavy.

"Why are you talking like some kind of guru?"

John ignored my sarcasm. "Do you see yourself becoming like one of those winos you were hanging around last night?"

"No way!"

"Why do you hang around them?"

"Nothing better to do."

"I used to work in a mission. A lot of the folks who asked for help were going through some kind of personal tragedy. But many came because their parents had gone to missions and their friends went to missions and other places where they could get free handouts."

I looked him in the eye. "Why'd you tell me that?"

"Why do you think I told you?"

I didn't say anything. Finally, "You told me because you think I'm gonna become like those winos I sometimes hang around with."

John snorted his characteristic snort. "I don't know what you'll become. I was just talking." The aluminum lawn chair he'd been sitting in creaked as he got up and went inside.

I didn't immediately change the company I kept. I couldn't. But as I learned to accept my situation and my attitude improved, I became more conscious of the type of folks I hung with and as I continued thinking about the type of people I wanted to influence me, my choice of who I kept company with gradually changed.

Chapter 14

Turning Negative to Positive

Better to light a candle than to curse the darkness.
—Chinese Proverb

Have you ever thought about the power of your thoughts? One thing I've learned since my injury is this: not only are negative thoughts destructive, they're also addictive. Luckily, the addiction to negative thinking can be treated like any other addiction.

To chase away the dark clouds of negativity, to turn my negative thoughts into positive thinking, to change limits to possibilities, these ten steps have worked for me. I offer them to you as a road map for happy travels.

(1) Commit yourself to positive goals.
(2) Say only positive things.
(3) Be patient with yourself.
(4) Hang out with positive people.
(5) Forgive yourself when you backslide.
(6) Eat healthy meals.
(7) Get physical exercise regularly.
(8) Keep track of your progress.
(9) Believe that God, or whichever Source, will help you succeed.
(10) Remember that Winners Don't Quit!

Following these ten steps helped me change my negative thoughts to positive ones. But I'm only human and humans love to hold onto their addictions. If you want to rid your mind of negative thoughts and a negative thought pops into your head, pop it back out by thinking of something positive. The more positive sayings you know and the more positive books you read, the easier it will be to replace that negative thought with something positive.

Although drivers in Seattle seem to manage it, most people's minds are never completely empty. I'm just kidding. If it wasn't for Seattle drivers, I probably wouldn't have gotten my license back. Luckily, I fit right into Seattle traffic. Everyone here drives like they're brain damaged.

Anyway, at least one thought is always on our minds. Because our minds cannot maintain a vacuum, we can't replace a negative thought with nothing. And it doesn't help to replace one negative thought with another negative thought. Therefore, we need a positive thought to replace it with.

The more positive thoughts and memories we store up from books or songs or friends, the easier it will be to let go of the negative and welcome the positive. And when we celebrate our abilities, we'll look for the possibilities in situations where we used to find limitations.

Remember, there are no limits.

Chapter 15

Breaking the Addiction

You always pass failure on the way to success.
—Mickey Rooney

It's one thing to stop doing something you're addicted to, but it's entirely different to stay stopped. So now that I've given you the steps I use to help chase away negative thoughts, let me share three choices that I try to make to keep away negative thoughts.

1) I choose to ask questions and not make assumptions.

When people do things to us, or say things, we automatically assume we know what these people are thinking or intending. We don't. We can only learn the truth by asking questions and seeking clarification. I used to assume that I knew what people were thinking about me, and why they acted around me the way they did. This made me feel angry, mean, and sorry for myself. "They don't like me, or they're out to get me," and other thoughts like these filled my head—all examples of negative thinking. It's no coincidence that in the dictionary the word "assume" is spelled: ASS-U-ME. In other words, assuming stuff makes an ass out of you and me. That's too perfect to be an accident.

For years my speech impairment made me feel so uncomfortable, I felt like I was the only guy at a bridal shower. After I got out of the hospital, I began to assume that all "normal" people thought I was a mental case because of my speech impairment. This was particularly disturbing since I enjoy talking so much. It's like keeping my mouth shut wasn't even an option. That solution never even occurred to me. By assuming I knew what people were thinking and that they were thinking derogatory things about me, I felt angry, depressed, and just plain miserable. Because I never asked what they were thinking, or if they were thinking about me at all, I'll never know if they even knew I was around.

It's entirely possible that all the negative emotions I was feeling were entirely of my own creation. One valuable lesson my journey has taught me is to not assume that I know what other people think of me.

My rehabilitation process has taught me other useful lessons. For example, stumbling around the block while holding my cane off the ground, repeating words and phrases into a tape recorder, learning to tie my shoes with one hand, and holding my water till I reach the bathroom, all taught me the same lesson: success is closest when my hope for tomorrow's victory is more important than my memory of yesterday's failure.

As I hobbled around the block holding my cane off the ground, my dream of one day walking without a cane kept me going. If my head had been full of memories of the last time I fell, I probably would have sat on the porch.

Having a poor memory can actually be a good thing. At least I had to buy only one CD. My memory used to be so bad that once I forgot I was paralyzed. I was walking around normal—until someone reminded me I was paralyzed. "Oh yeah, thanks," I said. And I began hobbling again.

Relearning to drive convinced me of another powerful choice. What you believe about yourself and your potential is more important than any so-called limitations and what other people think or say or do.

2) I don't take criticism personally.

Oscar Wilde once said about critics who wrote about his plays: "Criticism is a form of autobiography." He was right. Criticism reveals more about the critic than it does about the person or event being criticized.

Don Miguel Ruiz wrote, "Don't take anything personally." Nothing anyone ever says to you or does to you is about you. It is a projection of the feelings and reactions that are going on inside the person doing the criticizing.

Criticism used to bother me a great deal, even if I wasn't altogether sure it was directed at me. My self-esteem was so low that I automatically assumed that anything negative or derogatory was meant for me and was true. Two realizations helped me change how I perceived criticism.

(a) Even winners get criticized. But they can ignore it. They can evaluate its worth and discard what they don't believe has merit.

(b) Criticism is actually a gift. If someone gives you a gift and you refuse it, who does it belong to? Just because someone criticizes me doesn't mean I have to even acknowledge it. But since it's free, it would be foolish if I didn't choose to at least examine it to see if it has any value.

It has taken me many years and hundreds of choices, some good and some not so good, to reach a level where I can again consider myself a winner. The important thing is not that I made some bad choices. The important thing is that I kept making choices. Life is like selling vacuum cleaners. The more doors you knock on, the more times you open yourself up to failure—but the more doors you knock on, the more sales you are going to make.

3) Whatever I do, I always do my best.

I want to live without regrets about what might have been if only I tried a little harder. Life is like a boxing match. Sometimes you're fighting someone who is stronger, faster, and smarter. But you can still win. You've just gotta take his best shot and keep coming.

Like Jack Dempsey, who many consider to be an All-American boxing superstar, said, "A champion is someone who gets up when he can't." In other words, Winners Don't Quit!

Chapter 16

The Power of Hard Work and Patience

With time and patience the mulberry leaf becomes a silk gown.
—Chinese proverb

When I'm feeling happy and positive, I feel like there's nothing I can't do. Big deal! We all feel capable of conquering the world when things are going our way. But what about times when things aren't going our way? If you're like me, sometimes you feel depressed.

When I'm feeling that way, I do two things. First, I pray for help. Everybody has his or her own way of connecting with their personal idea of the divine, and that's as it should be. I think that what really matters is that you are connected with a power outside of yourself.

Alcoholic's Anonymous taught me how powerful it is to turn my life and my will over to the care of God as I understand him. I do not want to turn this line of thinking into a debate. I'm only saying that things seem to go much better when I trust God instead of trying to control things. For everyone who agrees, there's probably someone who disagrees. Oh well. Maybe if we had more accepting and trusting and less controlling, we could all be happier.

The second thing I do when I'm feeling down is look around and see how other people are handling their problems. Most folks don't go around talking about their problems. But if I show genuine interest in someone's situation, it's amazing how willing people are to share themselves with someone who will listen.

I've been the friend for the past ten years of a woman named Sharon, and I've learned a lot from her. When she's at work and dealing with customers, she's happy and cheerful. But when she is stressed from working overtime, she has no problem telling someone exactly what she thinks about something. When we first met, she lived in the same condo complex as I did. She was amazing. All by herself, with no help from the government or relatives, she not only raised her two kids to be responsible professional adults, she raised them to be happy, unselfish people.

What's even more amazing are the single parents all over the country who are motivated by love to do things for their children that would inspire anyone who really looked.

The woman I mentioned earlier, who was one of the last polio victims and as a single parent raised five kids, became a comedian after becoming a single parent. She used her love, her determination, and her comedy earnings to raise her kids without help from anyone. When her kids were raised, she could finally slow down. In her free time, she found and married a man with whom she's very happy. I love true stories like these.

To me, stories of people turning desperate situations into happy ones are springs of hope. When I hear a story of a person doing something ordinary people don't do, I feel empowered to do more than I thought I could.

Having been through years of rehab in Seattle's largest trauma center, I've seen dozens of situations that looked hopeless. I haven't kept track of everyone, so it's possible that some situations were hopeless. But I'm friends with a few former patients and I've seen their lives gradually and dramatically improve. I've seen first hand how powerful the human spirit is. My own situation seemed hopeless, but with patience and hard work, mostly patience, my situation has changed to one in which I'm now increasingly happy.

I have now been living with disabilities longer than I lived without them. Looking back on my last twenty-one years of rehabilitation, I can say truthfully that patience with my own situation is one of the most valuable lessons I've learned. Twenty-one years ago, I would have never guessed I would live to be as old as I am now. If I had realized sooner how much things could change for the better by applying strong efforts to improve, my journey would have been easier and a lot more fun.

Case in point: My dad came from Germany when he was eighteen and got a low paying job, but he wasn't content. By steadily applying himself, he learned the English language and went to college and then university. Because of his patience and hard work, he turned his situation into one that he and our family came to be proud of.

Chapter 17

There Are No Limits

The longer and steeper the climb, the better the view.
—Unknown

One of the best things about life is its consistency. When you do certain things, you get certain results. When my self-esteem was at its lowest, I used the law of cause and effect—not purposely. In fact, I used it to my detriment. But, detriment or not, by using it I proved that I still had some control over my situation. I would have been happier had I trusted that God as I understood him was going to work everything out. But at the time, I couldn't just sit there. I had to control something—anything.

Since my brain injury impacted everything, from my circumstances and emotions to my very body, the type of control I exerted was limited to trying to pull people into my life by being pleasant or pushing people out by being unpleasant.

Because being pleasant will pull people toward us only if they want to be pulled, pushing people away is much easier in terms of percentage of success. Without realizing it at the time, I was trying to restore a feeling of power over my limitations, so I did more pushing than pulling. I didn't understand this until years later. In trying to gain a feeling of power over my circumstances, I succeeded in pushing almost everybody out of my life.

Combine my excessive drinking with a need for power and what you have is a candidate for Alcoholics Anonymous. The in-patient treatment center I mentioned earlier gave me certain tools and a basic understanding of why I drank. But as the years passed and I gradually began feeling better about my circumstances and myself, my need to drink changed.

Alcoholics Anonymous kept me clean and sober for five years. I continued going to AA when I returned to Walla Walla College and that worked out fine. After being sober for a few years I decided to become a preacher and started going to a private seminary in California. Since spiritual people who were always talking about God surrounded me, I decided I didn't need AA. That mistake resulted in my beginning to drink again. Deciding to be a pastor was an impulsive decision, which I didn't have the commitment to complete. Instead, I returned to Seattle and made my second try at a four-year college. I've already mentioned how that went.

One night at a bar in south Seattle, I was given an open bar tab and I got sloppy drunk, totally unprofessional. Promising myself to go slow and be careful, I decided to ignore the bartender's advice and drive home.

The bar was close to the I-5 freeway and, once on I-5, I thought I was doing pretty well. I knew that drunk people like to speed, so I kept my speed at about 30 mph so the cops wouldn't notice me. Yeah right. I drove with my tires on the turtles separating the lanes, so I could tell if I was swerving or not. There wasn't much traffic, so it didn't seem important that I was using two lanes. A couple times I had to use all three lanes, but hardly ever.

Suddenly red lights flashed in my rearview mirror and a siren wailed. Uh oh. I pulled over and waited while the officer marched up to my car.

He took one look at me and pulled out his alcohol-breath tester. I spent two nights and three days in jail. They put me in the same cell as red uniformed felons! I saw at least two fights. I didn't see any weapons, but these guys were beating the stuffing out of each other. There was blood and broken teeth and handfuls of hair. I was freaking out! How'd I get in here? I haven't drunk and driven since.

Stand-up comedy gives me plenty of opportunities to receive free drinks, but doing stand-up comedy also gives me plenty of reasons to stay clean and sober. Comedy routines require all that I have to give and I function at a much higher level if I keep my head clear, which is why I've returned to AA. I sometimes miss drinking, but except for a temporary feeling of exhilaration, there is really nothing good that drinking ever did for me. Then why did I drink? Drinking blotted out reality and made me feel like I had control, among other things. Drinking gave me a sense of power. However, it turned out to be the power to destroy every aspect of my life— social, financial, physical, academic, and other parts.

I remember one time when my friend, Joe, and I—whom Cheryl and I had gone with to the Bruce Springsteen concert—went out drinking. As usual I drank way too much and when I went to the restroom, I ended up falling and cracking open my forehead on the (tile) floor. That's one example of drinking causing me social embarrassment and physical pain, although the pain didn't come till the next day.

I can't remember the combination of events that got me to AA, but I'm glad I made it. Some people don't make it. AA tells new people to come to ninety meetings in ninety days. I figured if ninety in ninety is good, 300 in ninety would be even better! AA was my social life. The beauty of AA was the worse I acted in AA, the more people who had been around a while would nod their heads and say, "Keep coming back." AA is a great program and I, and a lot of other lucky folks, owe AA credit for our happy and fulfilled lives. Thanks for everything, AA!

Another organization that helped me was a single's group that meets near my condo. They had a talent show in the summer of 1995. I wanted to be in it, but I didn't have any talent. I wondered, "What can I do to be in this talent show?" I know, I'll tell some jokes. Everybody likes to laugh.

The day came, and I got on stage and told some jokes. They were probably pretty lame (get it?). But people laughed and afterwards a girl came up to me and told me she was a former comedian and she said I had a "great stage persona." She didn't say she liked my jokes, but she took me to downtown Seattle to an open mike and I began doing stand-up comedy.

Over the years, projecting my voice into the microphone has improved my speech and increased my confidence. After doing comedy all over the Pacific Northwest, I started sharing my story in schools, elementary through university. I love doing stand-up comedy, and I'll always do it, but it's not nearly as fulfilling as motivational speaking at school assemblies and before corporate audiences.

Even though I took first prize in the 2000 Laff-Off at Giggles Comedy Club in Seattle, I decided it would be pathetic if all my injury meant was that I could get few laughs.

So I'm focusing my energy and attention now on delivering inspirational and motivational presentations, which has done a lot to forward my social and business skills. AA taught me to claim progress not perfection, and I'm making some incredible progress. Becoming better at interacting with others is a lot like doing stand-up comedy and mainlining heroin. The more you do it, the better you get (I'm kidding). I never did heroin. I'm brain damaged, not retarded.

Is your life a series of challenges or a series of calamities? Do you see only limitations or possibilities? It's your choice. Your choices have the power to make you who you want to be, but they also have the power to keep you from becoming the person you were meant be. Which will it be? It's your choice.

As a Chinese proverb says: "The person who removes a mountain begins by carrying away small stones." May each of your choices help you carry away another stone.

Now you know why I say, "There are no limits." When you accept the realities in your life with gratitude—and yet still believe in your dreams and possibilities—almost anything is possible.

MEET THE AUTHOR

Born in Detroit in 1961 and raised near Seattle, Al Foxx was a typical strong-willed, athletic teenager—until his life was changed forever in a motorcycle crash in 1980.

He earned his GED and quit high-school during his junior year so he could get a job to buy the things he loved. At that age, snow skiing and backpacking, cars and motorcycles were more fascinating than chalk boards and textbooks.

Al was hired as a hot tar roofer after the roofing company owner obtained permission from then Washington Governor Dixie Lee Ray for Al and a friend, neither of whom were 18, to be employed as roofers. The law forbids people not of legal age to be employed as hot tar roofers.

Al loved going to rock concerts in the 1970s. After leaving the house of his fiancée on his way to a spring concert in 1980, while speeding down the road, his bike crashed into a pickup truck that ran a stop sign right in front of him.

He spent the next month in a coma and woke up with a brain injury and the left side of his body partially paralyzed. Roofing was no longer an option. Al spent the next seven years in physical and speech therapy, and going to college. Fifteen years after his motorcycle crash, still limping noticeably when not using a cane, Al had graduated from Seattle Central Community College. He was going to Western Washington University when he realized college still didn't have anything for him. He devoted himself to stand-up comedy.

Al won first place in the 2000 "Laff-Off" at Giggles Comedy Club in Seattle. He enjoys poking fun at his disability and continuing stand-up comedy, but his heart is now in motivating students and adults, with humor, when he performs in school assemblies and in corporate settings. Thousand have now heard the lessons Al gained in rehabilitation. When asked how humor has helped him come to grips with his disability, Al replies, "When you laugh at something, it becomes less significant and easier to deal with. Laughter helps us realize that life has No Limits."

Printed in the United States
146741LV00003B/5/P

9 780978 378134